THREE MODERN JAPANESE PLAYS

THREE
MODERN JAPANESE PLAYS

Authorized Translations by

YOZAN T. IWASAKI
AND
GLENN HUGHES

With an Introduction by Glenn Hughes

c . 1

One-Act Play Reprint Series

Core Collection Books, inc.
GREAT NECK, NEW YORK

895.62
IWASAKI

First Published 1923
Reprinted 1976

International Standard Book Number
0-8486-2003-8

Library of Congress Catalog Number
76-40387

PRINTED IN THE UNITED STATES OF AMERICA

CONTENTS

INTRODUCTION

DURING the past quarter-century there have been many and varied attempts to interpret the East to the West. Through the media of philosophy, poetry, painting, drama, and allied arts, the Orient has made itself felt in a most striking manner among the Western peoples. And probably there is no one who will question the statement that the influence of Eastern arts will become even greater in the future.

Thus far the drama of the Orient, and of Japan in particular, has been interpreted to Europe and America chiefly through the translation of classical plays. The *No* drama is the most familiar, and its selection by translators has been caused, undoubtedly, by the fact that this type of drama is exceedingly old, and is the perfect flower of ancient Japanese civilization and culture. Poetic, dignified, stylized, and technically exquisite, the *No* represents a peculiarly true manifestation of the theatre of the East.

Unfortunately, however, these classical plays do not lend themselves to translation. The dialogue which composes them is so simple that it comes near vanishing altogether when it is forced into another language, and inasmuch as the production of the *No* depends so greatly upon dancing, costuming, and music, a feeble and inadequate impression of their power and beauty is obtained by the reading of an English translation.

Another point which must be made clear is that

INTRODUCTION

Japan has undergone during the past few years a dramatic as well as an industrial transformation. The theatre arts of Europe and America have reached the younger generation, and have brought new forms of play-construction and presentation to be set up beside the formal methods of the *No*, the *Kabuki*, and the *Doll-play*. Ibsen and Strindberg, Tolstoi and Shaw have carried their technical and philosophical revolutions into the East, just as a few years ago they carried them into England and the other countries of the West. It was according to perfectly natural and comprehensible laws that the wave of modern drama should strike Japan after it had struck shores nearer home.

But the realistic revolt, if we may speak academically, has certainly functioned and is still functioning in the East. Thesis plays, both foreign and native, have already been seen in Tokyo, and are still seen regularly there. They have not supplanted the older classical drama, but they have challenged it. And the present-day writers of plays in Japan reflect most interestingly the conflict of these different dramatic impulses and theories.

The three short plays which we have chosen to illustrate the new Japanese drama are different from each other, but they are all born directly of Western influences. "The Razor" is obviously an expression of industrial unrest, fashioned after the realistic psychological drama of Europe. "The Madman on the Roof" is in structure, if not necessarily in thought, distinctly Western. "Nari-kin", written in the United States, is purely Occidental in its conception and arrangement.

"The Razor", by Kichizo Nakamura, was first

8

published in *The Central Review* in 1914. Within one year it had been performed seventy-one times in the principal cities of Japan and Manchuria. This success was due to the vision and ability of the late Shimamura Hogetsu, a professor in Waseda University, who was the first man in Japan to found a modern art theatre. His co-worker, Sumako Matsui, a highly gifted actress who helped break down the native tradition against the appearance of women on the stage, appeared in the rôle of Oshika. These two ardent moderns considered "The Razor" to be the best modern one-act play in Japanese.

The author, Mr. Nakamura, is a pioneer of the new drama. He has not, however, devoted himself entirely to writing for the theatre. In fact, it was a novel which made him famous. With "The Pastor's House", a novel which still enjoys tremendous popularity, he won a prize offered by the Osaka *Mai-Nichi*, and since that time he has grown steadily in public favor as a writer. Besides "The Razor", he has written five other well-known one-act plays: "Meshi" (Rice), "Ridicule", "After the Strike", "Illusion", and "The Butcher-Shop".

Kan Kikuchi, author of "The Madman on the Roof", is considered one of the most versatile and clever writers in Japan. He is a successful novelist, short-story writer, and dramatist. Although still a young man, he is in great demand among Japanese readers, and is among the highest-paid contributors to magazines and papers. Critics classify him as an intellectual, and he is given credit for possessing a keenly analytical mind. His subject matter covers a wide range—from historical and legendary episodes to exceedingly modern dramatic conceptions.

"The Madman on the Roof" was published in 1919, and was produced in 1920 at the Imperial Theatre, Tokyo, with Kanya Morita in the role of Yoshitaro. Other successful plays by Kikuchi include: "The Love of Tojuro" and "Greater than Vengeance", both three-act dramas; and "The Father's Return", "The Son of a Revolutionist", "A Hero of the Sea", "The Wife Who Went on the Stage"—all one-act plays.

The third dramatist whose work is given place in this volume is Yozan T. Iwasaki, who is largely responsible for the translation not only of his own play, "Nari-kin", but of the other two plays as well. Mr. Iwasaki was born in Japan, received his education in Japan and in the United States, and for several years has lived in Seattle, where among other activities, he has directed the work of play-production on the part of Jiyu-geki-dan, a Japanese dramatic company devoted to the presentation of the world's best plays before their own people, in the Japanese language.

Here they have interpreted most admirably the finest works of Ibsen, Tolstoi, Strindberg, Shaw, and Hauptmann. From time to time they have gone to the new dramatists of Japan for material. Both "The Razor" and "The Madman on the Roof" have been played several times with great success, and Mr. Iwasaki has produced several of his own plays, one of them a three-act social drama of great power, called "The Price of a Wife," which is now being considered for production in Japan.

"Nari-kin", included in this book, was written in 1919, and was performed soon after. Since its first showing it has been repeated on more than one occasion, and has always met with great enthusiasm from the audience. In the original it has a vast amount of humor which it is not possible to retain in English translation; but the qualities of situation and characterization remain with sufficient effectiveness to suggest the interesting nature of the play.

It is possible that this volume will not convey to its readers a very satisfactory impression of the new plays of Japan, for it is even more difficult to be true to the form and spirit of Oriental literature than it is to give an adequate conception of the literature of Occidental countries other than our own. The idiom of Japan is often unrelated to our English idiom, and the whole background of Japanese thought, tradition, and manners tends to thwart those who desire to act in the capacity of interpreters for the Eastern and Western Worlds.

It is to be hoped, however, that some of the artistry, some of the clarity, and some of the dramatic beauty of these three plays will be revealed to those readers who are curious about the modern drama of Japan.

GLENN HUGHES.

University of Washington, Seattle.
May 6, 1923.

THE RAZOR

A Drama in One Act

by

KICHIZO NAKAMURA

(Authorized Translation,)

CHARACTERS

TAMEKICHI KIMURA, *a barber*

OSHIKA, *his wife*

HAYATA NOGUCHI, *Secretary of the County Office*

KEICHI SATO, *Principal of the grade school*

KANSHICHI, *son of a rich merchant*

SHUSAKU OKADA, *Councillor in the Department of the Interior*

PLACE: *A small village near Tokyo*

TIME: *The present*

THE RAZOR

The stage setting represents the interior of a village barber-shop. Three-fourths of the room is taken up by the zashiki—a raised platform about two feet high, covered with matting. In the center of the zashiki is a charcoal stove, upon which stand tea-vessels. In the wall at the back of the zashiki are two sliding screens. The entrance from the street is through another sliding door, also in the back wall, but to the right of the zashiki. Two shabby mirrors hang on the right wall. Under them, on a shelf, are combs, brushes, perfumes, soap, etc. In the upper right corner is a wash-stand. Two light, movable barber-chairs stand facing the mirrors. The atmosphere of the room is musty and stale. Dust lies everywhere. One bright-colored fan lying on the shelf is reflected in the mirror.

Tamekichi is discovered in his white work-jacket. He is busily engaged shaving a customer, and he appears much perturbed. His eyes flash nervously. Oshika sits on the zashiki by the charcoal stove, smoking a long Japanese pipe. She is about 27 years of age, and has charming eyes. Her hair is dressed in cho-cho (butterfly) style. A few wisps of hair hang down across her pale white face.

Noguchi is sitting on the edge of the zashiki reading a newspaper. He is about 25 years of age. He wears nickle-rimmed glasses, and his hair is cut in a short pompadour. He is dressed in a hakama— a skirt-like garment made of coarse material.

NOGUCHI

There will be a political speech at the Jyo-fuku Temple this afternoon, and tonight there is to be a reception. Well, he is a Representative in the House, and was appointed Councillor in the Cabinet. The newspapers are all talking about him, and so is everyone in the village. It is a good thing that today is Sunday, so that a lot of people from neighboring towns will be able to come and hear him. It is certainly an honor for our village to have a great man like Mr. Okada.

OSHIKA

Isn't he quite a young man still—about the age of my husband?

NOGUCHI

Perhaps in his thirties. When he is forty he may be Governor or Commissioner, and when he is fifty, he will be a Minister, I am sure.

OSHIKA

What! Is he really as great as that? What kind of looking man is he? I'd like to see him.

NOGUCHI (*laughing*)

Of course he is not handsome like an actor, but he has broad eyebrows, a tight mouth, and a dignified bearing. And then, he has piercing eyes— he sees through everyone.

TAMEKICHI (*laughing sarcastically*)

He is related to a mind reader.

NOGUCHI

This is not a joke. Yesterday he came to the County Office to inquire about taxation, and after he left, the Chief and the Treasurer talked about him. "His eyes are fearful!" they said. "There is something striking about his eyes. But anyway, he is very democratic, or he wouldn't have come down to the County Office himself." They admired him very much.

TAMEKICHI

Huh! Democratic! He went there for his own convenience.

OSHIKA

My husband went to see him yesterday, but Mr. Okada was too busy to receive him. This made my husband angry, but in our position we can't help it.

NOGUCHI

That's right. Even I have not been able to talk with him yet. I've only caught sight of him.

TAMEKICHI (*working on his customer with the brush*)

Of course there is a difference between the Secretary of the County Office and a Councillor in the Cabinet; but not between Shusaku and myself.

OSHIKA

You see, he and my husband were classmates in grade school. My husband graduated in first place, and Mr. Okada was second; so he thinks Okada is still his old-time friend. But the world doesn't go that way. I tell him not to think such things, or people will laugh at him. It really worries me.

TAMEKICHI

Which one of us will be laughed at—you or me?

NOGUCHI

The past is past. Now is now. If there is a difference between the Secretary of the County Office and a Councillor in the Cabinet, there is no relation at all between a village barber and a Cabinet

Officer. Mr. Tamekichi's queerness goes too far. Maybe it is the weather. (*He takes up the newspaper again.*)

OSHIKA

You are right! He is awfully disagreeable these days. Yesterday he tore up the newspapers that had the stories about Mr. Okada. He is crazy. I have to laugh at him.

TAMEKICHI

You talk too much nonsense. (*He glares at her, then takes the customer over to the wash-stand.*)

NOGUCHI

Ha! Here is a two-column story: "Okada, Councillor, comes home covered with glory." It's in big type, too. Well, whether a man is good or bad, unless he is worth a headline in the paper, his life isn't worth living. For otherwise he is not sure whether he is dead or alive. . . .

OSHIKA (*smiling with meaning*)

I got into the newspaper once.

NOGUCHI

Yes, yes. Over that suicide-pact. But you were young then.

OSHIKA

And now I am getting old.

NOGUCHI

No; I don't mean that. You are still beautiful. (*He is confused.*) Er . . . wasn't the man put in jail? You were lucky to get safely out of it.

OSHIKA

Yes, I am still alive, and am a barber's wife. No chance to get into the newspapers any more. It's better to keep out of the newspapers, anyway.

(*Tamekichi has finished trimming the customer's hair, and now comes and sits on the edge of the zashiki. He lights his pipe. Kanshichi, the customer, joins them and smokes also. He wears a summer kimono, with a grey silk waistband.*)

OSHIKA

Sit down, young master.

KANSHICHI

Thanks. (*He sits down.*)

NOGUCHI (*to Kanshichi*)

Iseya-san, stay a while, and as soon as I get my hair trimmed, I'll get even with you at chess. (*He hurries to the barber-chair and seats himself.*)

KANSHICHI (*to Tamekichi and Oshika*)

You are busy?

OSHIKA

No, not exactly. Come up and have a cup of tea.

KANSHICHI

Don't bother about me.

OSHIKA

No bother at all. Won't you come up?

KANSHICHI (*looking at Tamekichi, but speaking to Oshika*)

You are sure it won't disturb you? (*He climbs gingerly up beside Oshika near the stove.*)

OSHIKA

How is your wife? Is she getting better?

KANSHICHI

No; she is at her mother's; and I hope she doesn't come back. It is a terrible, life-long burden to have a sick wife.

OSHIKA

It is a pity for you to say such things.

KANSHICHI

I can't help it.

NOGUCHI (*laughs*)

Ha, ha, ha! You infected your wife yourself, and now you are trying to get rid of her. You are heartless. It must be a miserable thing to be the wife of such a man.

OSHIKA

Yes, indeed! But all men are selfish. You are no exception.

NOGUCHI

Why, everyone says Mr. Tamekichi is a loyal husband; but you seem discontented in spite of that.

OSHIKA

Of course I am.

(*Tamekichi watches Kanshichi out of the corner of his eye.*)

NOGUCHI

Say, Boss, when you finish your smoke, get my hair trimmed. I have to go to the Temple this afternoon and inspect the hall. I am very busy.

TAMEKICHI

You said just now you were going to play chess. Wait until I finish two or three more smokes. Don't get excited. I wasn't born to cut men's hair all the time.

NOGUCHI

But that's your business, so stop talking nonsense.

If you expect to live by barbering, you have to pay attention to your customers.

TAMEKICHI

Yes, I live off my eight-cent customers. (*Sarcastically.*) Many thanks!

OSHIKA

Don't be foolish! Get his work done. Of course it doesn't matter so much if you talk that way to Mr. Noguchi, but just the same, it hurts business.

TAMEKICHI

I am getting tired of this business. I want to quit.

NOGUCHI

Oh, don't do that, Boss. You are the only barber in town. If you quit, everyone will have to go to the next village.

OSHIKA

He talks that way all the time these days, and worries the life out of me. Young master, I wish you would speak to him about it.

KANSHICHI

Well, of course you have to work. (*He drinks his tea.*)

TAMEKICHI

Yes, we have to work, and the young master has to loaf. It is a well-arranged world!

OSHIKA

Don't put it that way. The young master is rich and doesn't need to work. He has plenty of money; his employes work for him, so it is all right for him to play around. Our fate is quite different from his.

21

TAMEKICHI

Huh! Your fate is unlucky! I am sorry.

OSHIKA (*laughing*)

Perhaps my marriage was unlucky.

TAMEKICHI

If you had been redeemed by the young master, you would be a lady of the Iseya family, and wouldn't need to even speak to a barber like me. You were foolish, all right to marry me. But as you were only a waitress in a tea-house, your present position is quite appropriate, and you had better be content with it.

OSHIKA (*her face flushing with anger*)

Don't say such things before the young master, you fool!

TAMEKICHI (*cynically*)

The young master hasn't forgotten you, at any rate. He still comes to see you occasionally. You had better thank him for that.

KANSHICHI

I am going. Here is the money. (*He throws a coin on the zashiki.*)

OSHIKA

Thanks . . . is it twenty sen? I'll get the change. (*She rises.*)

KANSHICHI

Keep the change. (*He gets down from the zashiki.*)

TAMEKICHI

Take your change. Here are twelve sen.

KANSHICHI

Never mind. I don't want it.

TAMEKICHI (*sternly*)

Yes you do. I have no reason to take more than the regular price.

(*Oshika hands twelve sen to Tamekichi, who holds it under Kanshichi's nose.*)

TAMEKICHI

Thanks!

(*Kanshichi takes the money and hurries out.*)

NOGUCHI

Boss, you are too outspoken.

TAMEKICHI (*looking after Kanshichi*)

Beast! (*With a backward look at Oshika.*) He's still thinking about her!

OSHIKA

Why are you so cross? We lose customers every day; and he is a very important one.

TAMEKICHI

Yes, important to you. But to me he is a sneak-thief, who takes a barber shop for a tea-house. Running after women—with his soft white face! There's not enough to him to pick up with chop-suey sticks. He eats, and produces nothing; but everyone respects him because he is a rich man's son. It makes me laugh!

NOGUCHI (*growing serious*)

That's right; just as you say. That kind of fellow we call a "bad egg". (*He looks around cautiously.*) We must be careful not to talk too loud, though.

OSHIKA (*smilingly*)

And yet I hear you used to go around the tea-houses with him, at his expense.

NOGUCHI (*confused*)

Well, of course . . . once or twice I went with him . . . for sociability. But I never made a fool of myself—for I have ambitions.

OSHIKA

Yes, I've heard for a long time that you were going to Tokyo to study. When are you really going to leave?

NOGUCHI

After I finish the correspondence course, I will study for a year or two more, and then take the examinations for the bar or the civil service. You can be sure I won't waste my whole life on this County Office Secretaryship. My superiors are always holding me down; and the only time I can show my importance is when I go to warn the delinquent taxpayers.

OSHIKA

That's just it. This spring you came here to warn us about paying our delinquent taxes, and you threatened to attach all our dishes and furniture and everything. You were quite a different person then; I was afraid of you.

NOGUCHI (*growing still more serious*)

I couldn't help performing my duty. At such times I am not myself. The power of our country's law takes possession of me; my natural feelings hide in some corner of my body, and I feel as though I had my hands on the pulse of other people. I enjoy seeing them suffer. But of course I am sorry afterwards, and am embarrassed when I see the same people again. (*He scratches his head comically, and forces a laugh.*)

THE RAZOR

TAMEKICHI (*laughing cynically*)

Yes, just as you say—holding their pulse. I practice that every day. Only mine is more than their pulse—a vital point. Thus I hold the razor in my hand, and shave men's necks. One slash of the razor would stop their breathing. And when I think of that, it seems to me that all customers are trusting fools. They don't know anything of what I am thinking, and they trust their throats in my hands, without suspicion. They let me touch their naked flesh with my razor as freely as I like. No matter what noble faces they have, or how eminent they are, or how proud, I have hold of their necks, and it is in my power to kill or to let live, according to the motion of one finger. So, whenever I finish shaving a man, I feel that I have saved a life, and I laugh to myself.

OSHIKA

Oh my! You mustn't think and say such crazy things! There is something wrong with you. You had better go see a doctor.

NOGUCHI

Do you think such things while you are shaving people? That is terrible?

TAMEKICHI

In the beginning I did not. Then I was very cautious, and I tried to shave without hurting people, for the sake of my trade. But as I grew accustomed to it I got tired of doing the same thing every day, all day long. Finally I reached the point where I could stand it no longer. I wanted to cut somebody's throat, so that I could quit this place. And ever since then, this idea has nested in my head;

25

when I shaved that youngster just now I thought I would thrust my razor into his throat.

OSHIKA

Oh! there is surely something the matter with him! What shall we do, Mr. Noguchi?

NOGUCHI

I can hardly trust him to shave me now. If I am killed here in the barber shop I can never rise in the world—and I have great ambitions. (*He moves to another chair out of Tamekichi's reach.*)

TAMEKICHI (*with a contemptuous laugh*)

My craziness doesn't make me cut the throats of county officials. For I would have to pay with my own life for such a deed. You are not worth it, any more than that youngster was. But if he had done something to my wife, he would never have got out of here safely, I can tell you that.

NOGUCHI (*with a sigh of relief*)

If there is no cause, then, you will not kill anyone.

TAMEKICHI

Well, if there were a cause, it would be only natural. Whenever I have finished shaving anyone safely, I wonder why it is that the razor slides so smoothly over his face. If this point were to get just a little under the skin, it would cut the cheek-bone, and the red blood would spurt out. Why does the razor always slide over the surface? Ha, ha, ha! I know. My hand has become a machine to trim people's hair and shave their faces. It is unbearable! I am still alive. And to prove I am alive, I would let the razor slip once. And yet, when I think it over calmly, something whispers to me that this would mean the exchange of my life.

OSHIKA

Mr. Noguchi! Why does he talk this way?

NOGUCHI

He has a rush of blood to the head. (*To Tamekichi*)
Say, Boss, you had better rest a little while.

TAMEKICHI

No. I am still considering my own life, so there is
no danger. But if I found the right person, I would
exchange my life, for to go on with this monotonous
business until I am a bent old man—that is awful.
But I never meet one who is worthy—only the
County Commissioner, the Village Mayor, and the
Postmaster. I couldn't cut their throats. . . .
A month ago a Major came here to inspect the
military drill, and he made a conceited remark
about a country razor not being sharp enough.
I thought of replying that if it wouldn't cut hair,
it would cut bones; and I came near thrusting
the razor into his throat. But I didn't do it; it
seemed too foolish.

NOGUCHI

So the County Office was saved the trouble of
settling that. It was a close call, though.

OSHIKA (*with a deep sigh*)

There is surely something the matter with him
these days. Please, Mr. Noguchi, don't repeat
these things to anyone. We might lose trade.

TAMEKICHI

So much the better if we lose trade! I have other
ideas. This isn't the only village the sun shines on.
It's a wide world.

OSHIKA (*soothingly*)

Of course the world is wide, but this is our only

way of making a living. We can't do anything else, no matter how hard we try.

NOGUCHI

What you say is probably right. (*He appears to think deeply.*)

(*Sato, the School Principal, enters. He is about 50 years of age, with grey hair and whiskers. He wears an old-fashioned short frock-coat, with silver chains on his vest.*)

SATO

Good-day. Ah, Mr. Noguchi! You are waiting to be shaved, too?

NOGUCHI (*very politely*)

No; I am in no hurry. You first, Professor.

(*Tamekichi nods to Sato.*)

OSHIKA

Welcome, Professor. Please sit down.

SATO (*speaking rapidly*)

Thank you, thank you. Mr. Noguchi, you are first. No need for you to be so polite.

NOGUCHI

No . . . I . . (*Faltering*) You go first, Professor. . . .

TAMEKICHI (*to Sato*)

Pray, sit down.

SATO

Thank you. How is business? Good, as usual?

TAMEKICHI (*heavily*)

Yes.

SATO

Mr. Noguchi is very busy these days, too, I suppose, with all the receptions, lectures, and so forth?

NOGUCHI

Yes. . . no . . . just a little inspection this afternoon at the Temple. There are a lot of committees, so I am not very busy.

SATO

Is that so? Well, at any rate today is a very joyous occasion. It is an honor to our village and an honor to our school.

NOGUCHI

Yes, indeed. Last year we celebrated the twenty-fifth year of your service, and this year we do honor to your pupil who has become a great man. So there is a double reason for rejoicing.

SATO

Indeed! It is a mutual pleasure. And Mr. Okada is as democratic as ever. He came to my house to see me last night, and we talked over old times. So today, as soon as I get shaved, I am going to repay his call. He leaves for Tokyo tomorrow evening. He is a very busy man.

NOGUCHI

Of course, as he is a high officer of the Central Government, time is important to him—even half a day.

SATO

That's right. And some day he will be a Minister. Well, he showed signs of greatness even in his schooldays. He always stood first or second in his class—never lower.

NOGUCHI

It is all due to his school training, so you are responsible.

SATO

Thanks, thanks! At any rate, from my pupil develops a great man. I feel very proud. That is the reward of a divine mission.

TAMEKICHI

Say, Mr. Noguchi, you come over here and sit down. Let's start on you.

NOGUCHI

No. Professor, you first. Any time will do for me.

SATO

No, no, Mr. Noguchi! First come, first served.

NOGUCHI

Later will be all right for me. You first, Professor.

SATO

But that would not be right. I came later than you.

TAMEKICHI

I'll finish either of you.

NOGUCHI

Professor, you please!

SATO

No. Courtesy is courtesy.

TAMEKICHI (*sharpening his razor*)

Then, Mr. Noguchi. I will stop your breathing first.

NOGUCHI

Don't joke! I'm in no particular hurry today. My hair isn't too long, anyway.

TAMEKICHI

All right, then, Professor, I'll finish you.

THE RAZOR

SATO

Excuse me, Mr. Noguchi. (*He crosses and sits in the chair. To Tamekichi.*) You are working hard these days. That is fine.

TAMEKICHI

Not exactly fine. This miserable business. . . .

SATO

Why, one trade is no better than another. All that is necessary is for each man to do his best in his particular business.

NOGUCHI

That's right, Professor. Mr. Tamekichi has stayed with this business a long time now; if he only keeps it up a little longer he will be all right.

TAMEKICHI (*examining the razor blade*)

What shall I keep up? (*He laughs loudly.*)

SATO

Everyone has a divine work to do, and he must keep up that work.

TAMEKICHI

You told me that same thing twenty years ago, and I have kept it up until this day. But now I am tired of it.

SATO

Yes, after your graduation you wanted to go to Tokyo to continue your studies; but your father was worried, and he asked me to advise you to follow his trade. And I agreed with him; so here you are. Now, isn't that fine?

TAMEKICHI

But you didn't advise Shusaku to follow *his* father's trade, and become a farmer.

31

SATO

But Mr. Okada had plenty of money, so I agreed that he should study in Tokyo. And that is what made him the famous man he is today.

TAMEKICHI

If I had had the money, then, I would not be a barber now. So it is money that makes men great. Ha, ha, ha!

NOGUCHI

After all, that's just it.

SATO

Well, Mr. Tamekichi was very good in school, too. I thought about you a great deal. But if you had rushed off to Tokyo you would have gone astray.

TAMEKICHI

I did run away to Tokyo two or three times, but my father always came after me and dragged me back home. Since then I have been a good-for-nothing, and have gone from bad to worse. Oh, I have tried to get over the idea, but I can't forget it. (*He resumes his shaving.*)

(*Noguchi returns to the edge of the zashiki and talks with Oshika.*)

NOGUCHI (*whispering*)

You had better keep an eye on him, Oshika-san.

OSHIKA

Indeed I will.

(*She moves forward and watches Tamekichi as he works. He sighs occasionally.*)

SATO

My whiskers are too thick—better shave them off.

TAMEKICHI

All right.

SATO

I am getting a lot of grey hairs, too.

TAMEKICHI

You can't help your age. But if you talk too much, Professor, the razor may slip, and I can't tell where I will cut you.

SATO

All right. All right. You scold me every time, but you have a razor in your hand, so I must do what you say.

TAMEKICHI

Better keep quiet; otherwise I can't handle the razor.

SATO

All right. All right.

(*Tamekichi is now shaving around Sato's throat.*)

NOGUCHI (*in a low whisper*)

I am in a cold sweat. If he presses down with one finger, that will be the end. How helpless human life is!

OSHIKA (*turning to Noguchi*)

Sh-h! He will hear you! If he gets excited, no telling what will happen.

NOGUCHI (*lying down on the zashiki*)

How helpless we all are! We go on madly seeking fame, wealth, success; but the pressure of one finger can end everything—and our life accounts are settled. After one is thirty it is foolish to go to Tokyo to study. Ah-h-h-h! (*He sighs.*)

OSHIKA

You are getting discouraged, Mr. Noguchi.

NOGUCHI (*excitedly*)

Without money one is powerless in the world!

OSHIKA

Yes, after all, it comes to that.

NOGUCHI

If he had the money, for instance, he might become Councillor too. You never can tell.

OSHIKA

Then I would be the Councillor's Lady! . . . But I have missed that destiny.

NOGUCHI

A woman can become famous without money. Her capital is a beautiful face and a fine body.

OSHIKA

If you look at it that way, then a man's capital is his arms.

NOGUCHI

Well, a man may have arms, but without money there is no hope for him these days. The times have made things that way. We can't help it. . . . (*He looks at Tamekichi.*) He is pretty near through. (*Muttering to himself*) I am going out for a minute.

OSHIKA

What about your haircut?

NOGUCHI

After a while. I have something to do right now.— Excuse me, Professor. (*He goes out hastily.*)

34

THE RAZOR

SATO (*coming back from the wash-stand, where Tame-kichi has taken him*)

Ah! I look younger.

OSHIKA

Professor, you always look well.

SATO

There are many things for me to accomplish yet in life, so I must keep strong and healthy.—By the way, give me a little perfume.

(*Tamekichi sprays him with perfume, then crosses to the zashiki. Oshika prepares some tea.*)

SATO

Has Mr. Noguchi gone? Oh, I am sorry I let myself be shaved first.

OSHIKA

No; he will be back soon.

SATO

Yes? (*He rubs his cheeks.*) I feel much better. When my whiskers grow I feel very strange; I can't tell whether it is my face or someone else's. But now it feels fine.

OSHIKA

Have a cup of tea. (*She serves it.*)

SATO

Thanks, thanks. Here is the charge. Good-bye.

OSHIKA

Get your change, Professor.

SATO

No; never mind. — Good-bye.

OSHIKA (*following him*)

Thank you very much. (*She turns to Tamekichi.*)

Tame-san, why don't you say "Thanks" or something? You are too rude.

TAMEKICHI (*blowing a cloud of smoke*)

No thanks necessary. — That old duffer! —
If Shusaku was remarkable in school, so was I.
I graduated in first place. Talking about "divine
work", and hanging on by his teeth to this one
job for twenty-five years without getting tired
of it. A patient fool, that's all!

OSHIKA

But that is just why the Governor rewarded him—
for his twenty-five years of patient service.

TAMEKICHI

Then I suppose I should wait for a reward from
the County Chief when I have finished twenty-
five years at the barbering business. Like hell!

OSHIKA

Don't lose your temper. That doesn't help matters.

TAMEKICHI

Well, I'm getting sick of this life, so it's only natural
for me to lose my temper. In the first place those
mirrors drive me mad. The same old dingy frames
that were there in my father's time. And if I look
in the mirror I see the faces of the men in the chair
changing every day—but the man who stands
beside the chair, in the white coat—his face never
changes. It is the same man always. Three hundred and sixty-five days in the year, the same
man with the same hands, going back and forth in
the same narrow room, repeating over and over
the same stupid things without a blush. It is a
glass prison! There is a man who cannot get out
of it for his life; and I feel sorry for him, I pity

36

him—but it is I, myself! I can't stand it! (*He pulls his hair.*)

OSHIKA

Well—that is our fate; so after all, we must be content with the three meals a day we get out of it. There is no other way—no matter what you think— so you may as well change your mind and settle down to work.

TAMEKICHI

I do work, but what comes of it? I work all my life like this, and support you. That is well enough for you. But is that the object of my life? Damned nonsense! You may like it, but I tell you I don't!

OSHIKA

Well then, can you tell me any other way? I don't say I like to spend my whole life here, being supported by you. I don't say I am contented with that.

TAMEKICHI (*sarcastically*)

Yes, when I see you entertaining the customers, I have an idea you are getting tired of it.

OSHIKA

Just as you say, I do get tired. Your customers change, but mine is always the same.

TAMEKICHI (*looking at her suspiciously*)

You mean that I am your customer?

OSHIKA

Isn't my husband the only customer that I have now? It wasn't so before.

TAMEKICHI (*spitting out his words*)

Huh! In the tea-house your customers changed

every night. But nowadays your customer's face never changes. So that is why you say you are getting tired!

OSHIKA

You just got through saying that the man's face in the mirror never changed, so I was reminding you of my own case.

TAMEKICHI

What are you reminded of?

OSHIKA

Don't be angry. I am serious, too, and sometimes I think the same things that you do.

TAMEKICHI

Think what things?

OSHIKA (*half laughing*)

When I wake up in the middle of the night, the same man is always sleeping beside me—and how dreadful I feel! (*Tamekichi stares at her.*) Ha, ha, ha! Don't look at me like that—with that terrible expression! I don't mean that I hate you.

TAMEKICHI (*collapsing*)

Ah! Man cannot trust anyone!

OSHIKA

Don't take it that way. You were talking about the mirror—I was talking the same way about my troubles. Everyone has to stand something.

TAMEKICHI (*his voice trembling*)

That's why these young toughs hang around here —because you are so frivolous. Even that Noguchi can't be trusted. None of the customers can be trusted! That alone is enough to make me hate

this business. I hate it! I'll smash that mirror!
(*He rushes across the room, Oshika following him
and holding him by the arm.*)

OSHIKA

Don't lose your temper. If you break up everything, what will you do tomorrow? Can't you
see we'll suffer for it?

TAMEKICHI

Let go! No matter how much we suffer—if we
die, that will be the end of it. Let me go! Let
me go!

OSHIKA (*clinging tightly to him*)

I don't want to die! If I wanted to die, I would
have died a long time ago.

TAMEKICHI

With whom would you have died? (*He turns and
stares at her.*)

OSHIKA

With anybody. No matter who.

TAMEKICHI

You harlot! (*He strikes her on the face, and col-
lapses in a chair.*) You said you loved me—but
you lied!

OSHIKA (*scornfully*)

Think what you like.

TAMEKICHI (*gnashing his teeth*)

I was fooled—and by such a woman! Am I such
a miserable creature as that?

OSHIKA

We are both miserable—you and I. We are a
good match. That's what you get for losing your
temper and crying. But there's no help for it.

(Tamekichi grovels in his chair, his hands to his forehead. The door opens and Councillor Okada enters. He wears a frock coat and silk hat, with a gold chain on his breast. In his hand is a cigar, from which a cloud of smoke is rising.)

OKADA *(smiling in salutation)*
Good-day.

OSHIKA *(bowing confusedly)*
Welcome.

(Tamekichi rises and looks vacantly at Okada.)

OKADA *(still smiling)*
It is I, Okada. It is a long time since we saw each other. I am sorry that last night when you called, I was busy with other guests.

TAMEKICHI *(his expression softening)*
Ah, Mr. Okada, you are welcome. *(He nods his head.)*

(Oshika goes hurriedly to the zashiki and arranges the things upon it. In her embarrassment she places the old dirty cushions for Okada, instead of the clean ones.)

OSHIKA
This way please, sir. Though everything is in bad shape.

TAMEKICHI
Please!

OKADA *(crossing in a dignified manner and sitting on the edge of the zashiki)*
Don't bother about me. I just came to pay my respects.

TAMEKICHI (*taking off his work-jacket and sitting on the zashiki, facing Okada. Politely*)

I am very happy to see you in my humble place, and I offer you my congratulations. (*He bows politely.*)

OKADA

Thanks. We haven't seen each other for a long time, but I am glad that you are getting along so well with your trade.

TAMEKICHI

No; everything is very bad—so bad that I am ashamed to have you see me.

OKADA

Nonsense, nonsense! All that can be asked of anyone is that he do well with his own trade. There is no honor in being an official. (*He puffs at his cigar.*)

TAMEKICHI (*with a bitter smile*)

But you are in an honorable position; while I am in such a miserable state that I am ashamed to talk with you. But I am thinking of quitting this business.

OKADA

Nonsense! Changing your trade wouldn't help matters any. You must be patient.

OSHIKA

That's right, sir, just as you say.

OKADA (*noticing her*)

Oh, I haven't spoken to you before, but I presume this is the wife of Tamekichi-san.

OSHIKA (*blushing*)

Yes, sir.—I have heard a great deal of you from Tamekichi. It is very nice of you to remember us.

OKADA

Well, Tamekichi and I were good friends in our mischievous school days. I often think of those times.

OSHIKA

Anyway, it is a great honor for us to have you visit us.

OKADA

Well, I must admit that I didn't make a special trip here. I was seeing a friend nearby, and I thought I might as well drop in and get shaved.

(*Tamekichi looks at Okada, his eyes lighting up.*)

OSHIKA

Oh, is that so? Then—get to work, Tamekichi-san.

OKADA

No hurry. I have nothing to do until afternoon. —When I came by the school building I noticed that the old black walls have been painted, but that the pasania tree hasn't changed at all.

TAMEKICHI (*coldly*)

Yes; some things change, and others do not.

OSHIKA (*laughing amiably, and speaking to Okada*)

Ha, ha, ha! You are the one who has changed most.

OKADA (*exultantly*)

I have not changed enough yet. I must break my cocoon two or three times more before I attain my desire.

OSHIKA (*flatteringly*)

Perhaps you will become a Minister.

OKADA (*laughing loudly*)

Ah, you are flattering me!—But a Minister is nothing. Someone suggested not long ago that Ministers should be appointed by throwing orange-peelings into a crowd, and making Ministers of those who are hit.

OSHIKA (*not knowing what to say*)

Er. . . . ah. . . . .

TAMEKICHI (*scornfully*)

It is not orange-peelings that are thrown, but money. One who has money can become a Representative or anything else; but the one without money is—a barber.

OKADA (*seriously*)

Tamekichi talks as though he really were tired of his trade.

TAMEKICHI

Tired nothing! I should have been born in a rich family, and been given a good education. Of course in grade school it doesn't matter: there is no difference between the poor and the rich. The strong boy is the leader, and the weak one a follower; the good student wins first place, the lazy student comes last. There's no complaint on that score.— And speaking of that pasania tree, Shusaku-san— I remember one time I picked acorns from it by standing on your back. It was a moonlit night.

OKADA (*reminiscently*)

Yes, yes. I remember that time. A bat flew out of a hole in the tree and frightened you so that you jumped down. I was frightened too, and tried to run, but stubbed my toe on a root, and fell on my nose, and made it bleed. I was thinking of that today. Ah, we were innocent in those days!

OSHIKA

My, my! Did such things really happen?

OKADA

It is very interesting to recall the days of our youth.

TAMEKICHI (*sighing*)

It makes me miserable. Mr. Okada has a future. Before me is darkness. I have lost my way. My hands and feet are bound.

OKADA

Why do you say such desperate things? If you work at your trade, isn't that satisfactory?

OSHIKA

There is a proper work for everyone, according to his own ability.

OKADA

Quite right. If one can support a wife and child, he is a real man, and has no reason to be ashamed.

TAMEKICHI (*laughing in self-contempt*)

I am sick of being "a real man"! Unless you become a great man or an utter fool, and can turn the world upside down, life isn't worth living. But to go on day after day with an existence as monotonous as a page of print, and not to be ashamed of it—that is not living at all. A man who does that is not a human being; he is a machine. I, myself, cannot tell sometimes whether I am using the clippers or the clippers are using me. It's a miserable thing!

NOGUCHI (*calls as he looks in at the door*)

Just a hair-cut. I have shaved myself. (*He enters,*

sees Okada, and is overcome with confusion. He bows embarrassedly.)

TAMEKICHI

Only a hair-cut, eh?

NOGUCHI

I am in no hurry.

TAMEKICHI

But you were first, so I will finish you up first. (*He puts on his work-jacket and comes down to the barber-chair. To Okada*) Just excuse me, will you?

OKADA

Yes, of course.

NOGUCHI

No!—Mr. Okada; you, please. Any time is all right for me.—Er . . . this is an unusual place for me to meet you. (*He bows rapidly and awkwardly.*)

OKADA

Go ahead, please. I am in no particular hurry.

TAMEKICHI

Mr. Noguchi has been waiting since this morning, so I will fix him up first. (*To Noguchi*) It's strange that you shaved yourself. (*Sneeringly*) No one would. . . .

OSHIKA

Do Mr. Okada first.

OKADA

It doesn't matter. (*To her*) If I wait, I can talk with you.

OSHIKA

Perhaps he can come to your house later, and shave you there.

OKADA

No, no! Don't go to that trouble. When I was abroad I used to shave myself every morning, and since I got married, my wife shaves me. But my razor got dull and I sent it out to be sharpened. Then I came down here, and haven't shaved for two days, so I don't feel very well with my face so rough.

(*During this time Noguchi has seated himself in the barber-chair. He leans back, and Tamekichi starts cutting his hair.*)

OSHIKA

So your wife shaves you? Is that so? (*She smiles.*)

OKADA (*looking closely at Oshika*)

I have seen you somewhere. Have you ever been in Tokyo?

OSHIKA

Yes; about ten years ago. But I never met you before.

OKADA

What part of Tokyo were you in?

OSHIKA

. . . Er . . . well . . . just in an out-of-the-way corner . . . . and for just a little while . . . I don't even remember very well.

OKADA

Is that so? Then it was my mistake.—Someone that looked like you. Ha, ha, ha! (*He laughs pleasantly.*)

OSHIKA

But Tokyo is a good city. It has changed a lot in ten years, I hear.

OKADA

It changes every day. Yes, Tokyo is the best city in Japan. Of course I'm not saying anything against my home town, but when I come here, I feel—cramped.

OSHIKA

That must be true. We would like to go to Tokyo to live. As long as you have to work hard anyway, it would be better to work in Tokyo. We get tired of the life here.

OKADA (*in a familiar manner*)

Come to Tokyo. That will be better for you. Why, if I stayed here a week I would get so I couldn't stand it. Of course I shouldn't say this, for after all it is my own district, and my parents live here.

OSHIKA

I agree with you. (*Showing her dimples.*) I should like to work in your house.

OKADA

Ha, ha, ha! That is excellent! If you were not married, I would take you with me. But as you are, I can't very well do it.

(*Tamekichi is listening to them carefully.*)

NOGUCHI (*crying out*)

Ouch! Don't cut my ear off! Be careful, Boss!

TAMEKICHI

I barely touched it. That's nothing.

(*Okada, interested in Oshika, leans forward on the zashiki.*)

OSHIKA

That needn't make any difference. If you have a

job for me, I'd like to go to Tokyo. So please don't think I'm joking. You find something for me to do there.

OKADA

Sure! My wife is sickly, and we need a housemaid; if you know of anyone for the place, let me know. I'm not joking. You keep it in mind.

OSHIKA

You mean . . . your wife is really sickly?

OKADA

Yes; female trouble. She has been suffering for a year now, in and out of the hospital. It is very hard on me. A woman ought to be strong and healthy. You look as though you were. (*He looks her over appraisingly.*)

OSHIKA

I am too poor to be sick; but really I am not very strong.

OKADA

Why, you are fleshy enough.

OSHIKA (*smiling*)

Maybe it is only fat. And besides, my color isn't good.

OKADA

Well, perhaps it is not so good where it is exposed, but in other places I imagine it is very good. There is no beauty in dark complexions, anyway. Ha, ha, ha! (*He laughs loudly.*)

OSHIKA (*simpering*)

You are very naughty, sir! Don't you tease me. If you say things like that to young girls, they will believe you and follow you.—Will you really hire me as housemaid?

OKADA (*playing with his mustache*)

It is hard to manage with a married servant. But if you hear of anyone else, let me know.

OSHIKA

I know of one. (*Fawningly*) There are some ashes on your collar. (*She leans over and brushes them off.*)

OKADA

Thank you. (*He looks over at Tamekichi, but speaks to Oshika.*) It will take him a little longer yet, and I am pretty busy this afternoon. Maybe you could shave me.

OSHIKA

I shave you? Oh, I never shave anyone except Tamekichi.

OKADA

I'm not afraid of your cutting me.

OSHIKA

All right, then.—Of course I won't shave you as well as your wife does.

OKADA (*laughs*)

But my wife hasn't shaved me for more than a year. (*He goes to the chair.*) Shall I sit in this chair?

(*Tamekichi looks askance at Oshika, and plies his scissors wildly. Oshika goes and puts the apron around Okada's neck.*)

OSHIKA

He is in a hurry, so I will shave him. Besides, he asked me to. (*She sharpens the razor.*)

TAMEKICHI (*harshly*)

I'll be through in a minute.

49

OKADA

I will trouble your wife; then it won't be necessary for me to ask my old friend to shave me.

(*Tamekichi looks away displeased.*)

OSHIKA

You are going away tomorrow, sir?

OKADA

Yes; I expect to leave tomorrow afternoon. I am a pretty busy man.

OSHIKA

I am sure you must be. So much coming and going must be awfully hard on you. And today you have a lecture and a reception. You must be tired.

OKADA

I am tired. But for the sake of their hospitality I mustn't say so.

OSHIKA

The newspaper has something about you every day. We quarrel over who shall read it first.

OKADA

Ha, ha, ha! They are always exaggerating. The Tokyo paper attacks me, and says I am traveling on Government funds to boost our party. All that kind of nonsense. You know.

OSHIKA

When you get back to Tokyo will there be a reception for you?

OKADA

I'm afraid not. Ha, ha, ha! This time there will not be a reception. But the reporters will mob me at the station. It's an awful nuisance. And then they pad up their stories with lies! Especially the opposition papers. Oh, it bores me.

OSHIKA (*touching him with the razor*)
I can't do as well as your wife. I am only a beginner.

OKADA
That's fine; fine!

(*Oshika smilingly rubs Okada's cheeks with her fingers, and looks at him in the mirror. At the same time Tamekichi combs Noguchi's hair roughly, and stares at the others out of the corner of his eye.*)

OSHIKA
You have a very thick beard.

(*Tamekichi takes Noguchi to the wash-stand.*)

OSHIKA
You have such beautiful hair. How I envy you!

(*Okada is silent. Tamekichi nervously pours perfume on Noguchi.*)

OSHIKA
What a beautiful border of back-hair you have! It is nice enough for a woman.

(*Okada is still silent. Noguchi returns to the zashiki, sees Okada in the mirror, and bows.*)

TAMEKICHI (*hastily sharpening his razor, his eyes changing color*)
Get out of the way, Oshika; I will shave him.

OSHIKA (*looking at him in surprise*)

Never mind. There is just a little more to do. (*In a lower tone*) Besides, he has dropped off to sleep.

NOGUCHI

Oshika-san, you had better do the shaving. The Boss is wild. He cut my ear.

OSHIKA

Oh, that's too bad! There is something wrong with him, all right.

NOGUCHI

It's even dangerous to let him use the scissors. I was uneasy, I can tell you.

OSHIKA (*with a little laugh*)

Noguchi-san, you are too easily frightened.

TAMEKICHI (*finishes sharpening the razor, feels of its edge, and smiles maliciously*)

The razor is not going to use me; I am going to use it.

OSHIKA

Never mind. I will finish him. It is all done but the throat.

TAMEKICHI

Get out! (*He glares at her.*)

OSHIKA

Never mind, I say! (*In a lower tone*) He is sleeping so nicely!

TAMEKICHI

Get out! (*He takes her roughly by the arm and pulls her away.*)

OSHIKA

Don't be so rough!—I am afraid he will wake up.

(*Tamekichi takes her place, and begins rubbing Okada's throat.*)

OKADA

Ah, you, Tamekichi?—I was having a good sleep, and was dreaming.

TAMEKICHI (*coldly*)

Perhaps you were dreaming of great fame and power.

OKADA

Well, I dreamed that I got a telegram and returned to Tokyo. Then I was invited to a wonderful palace, where there was a great hall with walls of gold hung with red velvet. The floor was a checker-board of black and white marble. —It was something like a palace that I saw when I was abroad.

TAMEKICHI

Huh! I can't even dream of such things!

OKADA (*as if talking to himself*)

And there was a marble platform with three steps leading up to it, covered with a beautiful carpet. —On the throne sat a queen wearing purple robes embroidered with gold.—And it was very funny about the queen.

TAMEKICHI (*sarcastically*)

Eh? How, funny?

OKADA (*laughing*)

Yes; it was very funny.—She resembled your wife! —I never had such a funny dream. I am sorry I woke up.

(*Oshika smiles at Okada in the mirror.*)

TAMEKICHI

Huh! The queen resembled my wife, did she? That *is* funny! (*He starts shaving Okada.*)

OSHIKA

You must be very careful. He is an important man.

TAMEKICHI (*turning upon her quickly*)

Who is important? You shut up!

OSHIKA

He's an important man, I say. Don't be as rough as you were on Mr. Noguchi.

TAMEKICHI

You make too much noise. Keep your mouth shut! (*He looks in the mirror and sees himself. Dramatically*) There he is! The same as ever! Working in his prison as he always is. He is a prisoner in a white coat, that fellow! . . . . (*He remains staring at his reflection.*)

OKADA

What are you talking about?

TAMEKICHI

I see myself in the glass, and I am beginning to feel sad. That is what I am talking about.

OKADA

Well, what of it?

TAMEKICHI

Shusaku-san is dreaming of luxury, and of another man's wife in purple robes. While I stand beside him, shaving, and breathing the bad odors of other men. I can't stand it! I can't stand it!

OKADA

You are getting a little nervous.

TAMEKICHI

Now there are two figures reflected in the mirror. But when Shusaku-san goes away, I will be left here alone. Left here alone in this prison forever. I can't bear it!

OSHIKA (*coming over near him*)

What are you saying? You had better hurry and finish shaving him. He's a busy man.

TAMEKICHI

Chatterbox! You said you wanted to go away with him!

OSHIKA (*with a bitter smile*)

Don't take that seriously. You are nothing but a big child.

OKADA

He seems awfully nervous. (*To Tamekichi*) Why don't you hurry and finish with me?

TAMEKICHI (*growing excited*)

Yes! I will finish!—I hold the razor in this hand, and your throat in the other hand. Now I fear no man in the whole world. Even a Minister or a General would be helpless. There is no one more powerful than I. Until this moment I was slave to the razor, and was prisoner in the mirror; and I suffered and was afraid.—Fool! I am still alive! And today I am master of the razor!

(*The blade flashes. Okada screams, and falls to the floor, the chair tumbling over with him.*)

OSHIKA

Oh-h-h-h! What have you done? (*She screams.*)

55

NOGUCHI

At last he has done it! (*His voice trembles.*) And there will be no lecture or reception!

TAMEKICHI (*staring vacantly into space*)

Ha, ha! Ha, ha! It is my body that lies before me! (*He laughs madly.*) Behold! Justice! (*He stands trembling—his face pale.*)

CURTAIN

THE MADMAN ON THE ROOF

A Play in One Act

by

KAN KIKUCHI

(Authorized Translation)

CHARACTERS

YOSHITARO KATSUSHIMA, *the madman, 24 years of age*
SUEJIRO KATSUSHIMA, *his brother, a 17-year-old high
    school student*
GISUKE KATSUSHIMA, *their father*
OYOSHI KATSUSHIMA, *their mother*
TOSAKU, *a neighbor*
KICHIJI, *a man-servant, 20 years of age*
A PRIESTESS, *about 50 years of age*

PLACE: *A small island in Sanuki Strait*
TIME: *1900*

THE MADMAN ON THE ROOF

The stage-setting represents the backyard of the Katsushimas, who are the richest family on the island. A bamboo fence prevents one from seeing more of the house than the high roof, which stands out sharply against the rich greenish sky of the southern island summer. At the left of the stage one can catch a glimpse of the sea shining in the sunlight.

Yoshitaro, the elder son of the family, is sitting astride the ridge of the roof, and is looking out over the sea.

GISUKE (*speaking from within the house*)

Yoshi is sitting on the roof again. He will get a sunstroke—the sun is so terribly hot. (*Coming out.*) Kichiji!—Where is Kichiji?

KICHIJI (*appearing from the right*)

Yes! What do you want?

GISUKE

Bring Yoshitaro down. He has no hat on, up there in the hot sun. He will get a sunstroke. How did he get up there, anyway? From the barn? Didn't you put wires around the barn roof as I told you to the other day?

KICHIJI

Yes; I did exactly as you told me.

GISUKE (*coming through the gate to the center of the stage, and looking up to the roof*)

I don't see how he can stand it, sitting on that hot slate roof. (*He calls.*) Yoshitaro! You better come

59

down. If you stay up there you will get a sun-stroke, and maybe die.

KICHIJI

Young master! Come on down. You will get sick if you stay there.

GISUKE

Yoshi! Come down quick! What are you doing up there anyway? Come down, I say! (*He calls loudly.*) Yoshi!

YOSHITARO (*indifferently*)

Wha-a-at?

GISUKE

No "whats"! Come down right away. If you sit in the hot sun you will get a sunstroke. Come on now—hurry! If you don't come down, I'll get after you with a stick.

YOSHITARO (*protesting like a spoiled child*)

No; I don't want to. Something interesting. The priest of the Konpira God is dancing in the clouds. Dancing with an angel in pink robes. They are calling to me to come. (*Crying out ecstatically.*) Wait! I am coming!

GISUKE

If you talk like that you will fall, as you did the other day. You are already crippled and insane. How you worry your parents! Come down, you fool!

KICHIJI

Master, don't get so angry. The young master will not obey you. Better get some bean-cakes; when he sees them he will come down, because he likes them.

GISUKE

No; you had better get the stick after him. Don't
be afraid to give him a good shaking-up.

KICHIJI

That's too cruel. The young master doesn't understand anything. He's under the influence of evil
spirits.

GISUKE

We may have to put bamboo guards on the roof
to keep him down from there.

KICHIJI

Whatever you do won't keep him down. Why,
he climbed the roof of the Honzen Temple without
even a ladder; a low roof like this one is the easiest
thing in the world for him. I tell you it's the evil
spirits that make him climb. Nothing can stop
him.

GISUKE

You may be right; but he worries me to death.
If we could only keep him in the house it wouldn't
be so bad, even though he is crazy; but he is always
climbing up to high places. That makes a show of
his insanity. Suejiro says that the Madman of
Katsushima is known to everyone as far as Taka-
matsu.

KICHIJI

Everyone on the island says he is under the influence of the evil fox-spirit, but I don't believe
that, for I never heard of a fox climbing trees.

GISUKE

I agree with you. And I have another idea. About
the time Yoshitaro was born, I bought a very
expensive imported rifle, and with it I killed every

monkey on the island. Now I believe the monkey-spirit is working in him.

KICHIJI

That's just what I think. Otherwise how could he climb trees so well? He can climb anything without a ladder. Even Saku, the professional ladder-climber, admits that he is no rival of Yoshitaro.

GISUKE (*with a bitter laugh*)

Don't joke about it! It is no joking matter, having a son who is always climbing on the roof. My wife and I worry over him every minute. (*Calling again.*) Yoshitaro, come down! Yoshitaro! Down, I say! —When he is up there on the roof, he doesn't hear me at all—he is so engrossed. I cut down all the trees around the house so he couldn't climb them, but there is nothing I can do about the roof.

KICHIJI

When I was a youngster I remember there was an *icho* tree in front of the gate.

GISUKE

Yes; that was one of the biggest trees on the island. And one day Yoshitaro climbed clear to the top of it. He sat out on a limb, at least ninety feet above the ground, dreaming away as usual. My wife and I never expected him to get down alive, but after a while down he slid safely. We were all too astonished to speak.

KICHIJI

Oh, my! That was a miracle.

GISUKE

That's why I say it is the monkey-spirit that works

in him. (*He calls again.*) Yoshi! Come down!
(*Dropping his voice.*) Kichiji, you had better go
up and fetch him.

KICHIJI

But when anyone else climbs up there, the young
master gets angry.

GISUKE

Never mind his getting angry. Pull him down.

KICHIJI

All right. All right.

(*Kichiji goes out after the ladder. Tosaku, the neighbor, enters.*)

TOSAKU

Good-day, sir.

GISUKE

Good-day. Fine weather. How about the nets
you put out yesterday. Catch anything?

TOSAKU

No; not very much. The season is over.

GISUKE

Is that so? Maybe it *is* too late now. But perhaps
you will catch some *hatsu* fish.

TOSAKU

Seikichi caught two or three of them yesterday.

GISUKE

Is that so?

TOSAKU (*looking up at Yoshitaro*)

Your son is on the roof again.

GISUKE

Yes; he is up there as usual. I don't like it, but when
I keep him locked in a room he is as unhappy as a

fish out of water. Then, when I think that is too cruel, and let him out, back he goes up on the roof.

TOSAKU

But then, he doesn't bother anyone.

GISUKE

He bothers us. We feel very much ashamed when he climbs up high that way, and talks so loud.

TOSAKU

But your younger son, Sue-san, has a good reputation at school. That is some consolation for you.

GISUKE

Yes; he is an unusually good student, and is some consolation to me. If both of them were insane, I don't know how I could stand it to go on living.

TOSAKU

By the way, a Priestess has just come to the island. How would you like to have her pray for your son?—That is really what I came to see you about.

GISUKE

Is that so? Well, we have tried prayers several times before, but it has never done any good.

TOSAKU

The Priestess who is here now believes in the Konpira God. She is very miraculous. People say she is inspired by the Konpira God, so that her prayers are quite different from those of a mountain priest. Why don't you try her once?

GISUKE

Well, we might. How much does she charge?

TOSAKU

Oh, she won't take any pay unless the patient is

64

cured. But if he is cured, then you pay her whatever you feel like.

GISUKE

Suejiro says he doesn't believe in any prayers. . . . But there isn't any harm in letting her try.

(*Kichiji enters carrying the ladder, and disappears behind the fence.*)

TOSAKU

Then I will go to Kinkichi's house and bring her here. In the meantime you get your son down off the roof.

GISUKE

All right. Thanks for your trouble. (*After seeing that Tosaku has gone, he calls again.*) Yoshi! Be quiet now and come down.

KICHIJI (*who is up on the roof by this time*)

Now then, young master, come down with me. If you stay up here any longer you will have a fever tonight.

YOSHITARO (*drawing away from Kichiji as a Buddhist might from a heathen*)

Don't touch me! The angels are beckoning to me. This is not a place where you can come. What do you mean by it?

KICHIJI

Don't talk nonsense! Please come down.

YOSHITARO

If you touch me the fairies will destroy you!

(*Kichiji hurriedly catches Yoshitaro by the shoulder and pulls him to the ladder. Yoshitaro suddenly becomes gentle.*)

KICHIJI

Don't make any trouble now. If you do you will
fall and hurt yourself.

GISUKE

Be careful.

(*Yoshitaro comes down to the center of the stage,
followed by Kichiji. Yoshitaro is lame in his right
leg.*)

GISUKE (*calling*)

Oyoshi! Come out here a minute.

OYOSHI (*from within*)

What do you want?

GISUKE

I have sent for the Priestess. What do you think
about it?

OYOSHI (*appearing at the gate*)

That may be a good idea. You never can tell
what may help him.

KICHIJI

Some of them do good, and some don't.

GISUKE

Yoshitaro says he talks with the Konpira God.
Well, this Priestess is a follower of the Konpira
God, so she ought to be able to help him.

YOSHITARO (*looking uneasy*)

Father! Why did you bring me down? There
was a beautiful cloud of five colors rolling down
to fetch me.

GISUKE

Foolishness! The other day you said there was a
beautiful cloud of five colors rolling down, and

you jumped off the roof. That's the way you broke your leg. Now today the Priestess of the Konpira God is coming here to drive the evil spirit out of you, so don't you go up on the roof, but stay here.

(*Tosaku enters, leading the Priestess. She has a cunning look.*)

TOSAKU

This is the lady I spoke to you about.

GISUKE

Ah, good-afternoon! You are welcome.—This boy is a great worry, and causes us much shame.

PRIESTESS (*casually*)

Don't worry about him. I will cure him immediately with the help of the God. (*Looking at Yoshitaro.*) This is the one?

GISUKE

Yes. He is twenty-four years old, and can do nothing but climb up to high places.

PRIESTESS

How long has he been this way?

GISUKE

Ever since he was born. Even when he was a baby, he wanted to be climbing. When he was four or five years old he climbed onto the low shrine, then onto the high shrine of Buddha, and finally onto a very high shelf. When he was seven or eight he began climbing trees. At fifteen or sixteen he climbed to the top of mountains, and stayed there all day long, where he says he talked with fairies and with gods, and such things. What do you think is the matter with him?

PRIESTESS

There's no doubt but that it is the evil fox-spirit. All right, I will pray for him. (*Looking at Yoshitaro.*) Listen now! I am the messenger of the Konpira God of this island. And all that I say comes from the God.

YOSHITARO (*uneasily*)

You say the Konpira God? Did you ever see him?

PRIESTESS (*staring at him*)

Don't say such sacrilegious things! The God cannot be seen.

YOSHITARO (*exultantly*)

Oh, I have seen him many times! He is an old man with white robes and a golden crown. He is my best friend.

PRIESTESS (*taken aback at this assertion, and speaking to Gisuke*)

This is the evil fox-spirit, all right, but a very extreme case. Now then, I will ask the God.

(*She chants a prayer in a ridiculous manner. Yoshitaro, held fast by Kichiji, watches the Priestess blankly. She works herself into a frenzy, and falls to the ground in a faint. Presently she rises to her feet and looks about her strangely.*)

PRIESTESS (*in a changed voice*)

I am the Konpira God residing in this island!

(*All except Yoshitaro fall to their knees with exclamations of reverence.*)

PRIESTESS (*with affected dignity*)

The elder son of this family is under the influence

68

of the evil fox-spirit. Hang him up on the branch of a tree and purify him with the smoke of green pine-needles. If you doubt what I say, you are all condemned!

(*She faints again. There are more exclamations of astonishment.*)

PRIESTESS (*rising and looking about her as though unconscious of what has taken place*)
What has happened? Did the God speak?

GISUKE
It was miraculous. The God answered.

PRIESTESS
Whatever the God told you to do, you must do at once, or be condemned. I warn you for your own sake.

GISUKE (*hesitating somewhat*)
Kichiji, you may go and get the green pine-needles.

OYOSHI
No! It is too cruel, even if it is the command of the God.

PRIESTESS
He will not suffer—only the fox-spirit within him. He himself will not suffer at all. So make haste! (*Looking fixedly at Yoshitaro.*) Did you hear the God's command? Leave the body of this boy before you suffer?

YOSHITARO
That was not the voice of the Konpira God. He wouldn't listen to a priestess like you!

PRIESTESS (*as though insulted*)
I will get even with you. Just wait! Don't you talk back to the God like that, you wretched fox!

(*Kichiji enters with an armful of green pine-needles Oyoshi becomes frightened.*)

PRIESTESS

You must respect the God or be condemned.

(*Gisuke and Kichiji rather reluctantly set fire to the pine-needles, then bring Yoshitaro to the fire. He struggles against being held in the smoke.*)

YOSHITARO

Father! What are you doing? I don't like this! I don't like this!

PRIESTESS

That is not his own voice speaking. It is the voice of the fox within him. And it is only the fox that suffers.

OYOSHI

But it is cruel!

(*Gisuke and Kichiji attempt to get Yoshitaro's face into the smoke. Suddenly Suejiro's voice is heard within the house.*)

SUEJIRO

Father! Mother! I am home!

GISUKE (*letting go his hold of Yoshitaro in consternation*)

Sue is home! Today is not Sunday. What is he doing home today?

(*Suejiro appears in the gateway. He wears a high-school uniform, and is a dark-complexioned, active boy. He stands amazed at the scene before him.*)

SUEJIRO

What's the matter, Father?

GISKE (*confused*)

What?

SUEJIRO

What is the meaning of this smoke?

YOSHITARO (*coughing from the smoke, and looking at his brother as at a savior*)

That you, Sue? Father and Kichiji have been putting me in the smoke.

SUEJIRO (*angrily*)

Father! What foolish thing are you doing? Haven't I told you time and again about this sort of business?

GISUKE

But the miraculous Priestess, inspired by the God of ——

SUEJIRO (*interrupting*)

Rubbish! You do these foolish things merely because he is so helpless. (*He looks contemptuously at the Priestess and crosses over and stamps the fire out with his feet.*)

PRIESTESS

Wait! That fire was made at the command of the God!

(*Suejiro sneeringly puts out the last spark.*)

GISUKE (*more courageously*)

Suejiro, I have no education, and you have, so I am always willing to listen to you. But this fire was made at the God's command, and you mustn't stamp on it.

71

SUEJIRO

Smoke won't cure him. People will laugh at you for talking about the fox-spirit. Why, if all the gods in the country were called upon together, they couldn't cure even a cold. This Priestess is an impostor! All she wants is the money—

GISUKE

But the doctors can't cure him.

SUEJIRO

When the doctors can't cure him, no one can. I've told you before that he doesn't suffer. If he did, we would have to do something for him. But as long as he can climb up on the roof, he is happy from morning till night. There is no one in the whole country as happy as he is—perhaps no one in the world. Besides, if you cure him now, what can he do? He is twenty-four years old and knows nothing—not even the alphabet; and he has had no experience. If he were cured, he would be conscious of being crippled, and would be the most miserable man in the country. Is that what you want to see? It's all because you want to make him normal. But isn't it foolish to become normal merely to suffer? (*Looking sidewise at the Priestess.*) Tosaku-san, if you brought her here, you had better take her away.

PRIESTESS (*angry and insulted*)

You disbelieve the oracle of the God. You are condemned! (*She starts her chant as before. She faints, rises, and speaks in a changed voice.*) I am the great Konpira God! What the brother of the patient says, springs from his own selfishness, for

72

when his brother is cured, the estate of the family will go to him—don't forget that. . . .

SUEJIRO (*excitedly knocks the Priestess down*)
It's a damned lie, you old fool! (*He kicks her two or three times.*)

PRIESTESS (*getting to her feet and resuming her ordinary voice*)
Ouch! Ouch! What are you doing? You wretch!

SUEJIRO
You fraud! You swindler!

TOSAKU (*coming between them*)
Now, young man, wait! Don't lose your temper.

SUEJIRO (*still excited*)
You liar! A woman like you can't understand brotherly love!

TOSAKU
Well, we'll go home right away. It was my mistake that I brought you here.

GISUKE (*giving Tosaku some money*)
Maybe you will excuse him. He is young and he has such a temper.

PRIESTESS
You kicked me when I was inspired by the God. Such a wicked fellow will be lucky to live until tonight.

SUEJIRO
Liar!

OYOSHI (*soothing Suejiro*)
Be quiet now. (*To the Priestess*) I am very sorry for you.

73

PRIESTESS (*going out with Tosaku*)
The foot you kicked me with will soon decay!

(*The Priestess and Tosaku go out.*)

GISUKE (*to Suejiro*)
Aren't you afraid of being punished for what you have done?

SUEJIRO
A god never inspires a woman like that old swindler. She lies about everything.

OYOSHI
I suspected her from the very first. If she was inspired by a real god, she wouldn't do such cruel things.

GISUKE (*without any insistence*)
Maybe so. But, Sue, your brother will be a burden to you all your life.

SUEJIRO
It will be no burden at all. When I become successful, I will build a high tower on top of Mount Takanoshiro, and there he can live.

GISUKE (*suddenly*)
But where has Yoshitaro gone, anyway?

KICHIJI (*pointing at the roof*)
He is up there.

GISUKE (*having to smile*)
As usual.

(*During the preceding excitement, Yoshitaro has slipped away and climbed back up on the roof. The four persons below look at each other and smile.*)

SUEJIRO

A normal person would be angry with you for having put him in the smoke; but you see, he has forgotten everything. (*He calls.*) Brother!

YOSHITARO (*as brotherly affection springs from his heart*)

Suejiro! I asked the Konpira God, and he says he doesn't know her!

SUEJIRO (*smiling*)

You are right. The God will inspire you instead of a Priestess like her.

(*Through a rift in the clouds, the golden light of sunset strikes on the roof.*)

SUEJIRO (*exclaiming*)

What a beautiful sunset!

YOSHITARO (*his face lighted by the sun's reflection*)

Sue, look! Can't you see a golden palace in yonder cloud? There! There! Can't you see? Just look! How beautiful!

SUEJIRO (*as he feels the sorrow of sanity*)

Yes, I see. I see it, too. Wonderful.

YOSHITARO (*filled with joy*)

There! From within the palace I hear the music of flutes—which I love best of all! Is it not beautiful?

(*The parents have gone into the house. The mad brother on the roof, and the sane brother on the ground, remain looking at the golden sunset.*)

CURTAIN

NARI-KIN

A Farce in One Act and Two Scenes
by
YOZAN T. IWASAKI

(Authorized Translation,)

CHARACTERS

MATSUZO HONDA, *an old man*
YOKICHI HONDA, *his son, 26 years of age*
OSHINA, *his daughter, 18 years of age*
TOMEGORO, *a laborer*
MITSUMURA, *owner of a shirt factory*
CHIKAKO, *his wife*
TAMAI, *his factory manager*

PLACE: *Osaka*
TIME: *The Present*

NARI-KIN*

SCENE I

The dwelling of Matsuzo Honda, in the poor quarter of Osaka. The entire stage is taken up with the zashiki, or that portion of a room which is elevated above the general floor level. There is an entrance at the left. The room contains a screen, a shelf, a charcoal stove, etc., but is very simple, and creates an atmosphere of poverty and gloom.

It is afternoon. When the curtain rises, the old man is cooking at the charcoal stove. Yokichi enters.

YOKICHI

Father, here I am.

MATSUZO

You are early this evening. What's the matter? Has anything happened?

YOKICHI

Yes, I think we are going on strike.

MATSUZO

What's that? You are going on strike?

YOKICHI

Yes, we sent a committee to negotiate with the employers about extra night work, but they refuse to pay overtime, so now everyone is mad, and unless they come through, we will strike. The manager of the company, though, is very sym-

---

*A term corresponding roughly to the French *nouveaux-riches*, and used in Japan especially to designate war-profiteers.

79

pathetic with us workers, and has promised to arbitrate for us. He asked us to wait until ten o'clock tomorrow morning.

MATSUZO

Is that so? Well, then, I think everything will be settled all right. (*He pauses.*) The manager is that young man back from America?

YOKICHI

Yes, that is the one. I told you about him the other day, didn't I? (*He pauses.*) You know in America the working people have more rights than we have here; so he is naturally sympathetic toward the workers, even though he is very young.

MATSUZO (*arranging the supper, and carrying the cooked fish to the small table, center*)

Is that right? If he is such a fine young man, it would be a good thing to have him marry our Oshina.

YOKICHI (*without enthusiasm*)

No, father. No chance of that. He's out of our class. We are poor men working for the company, and he's our manager. He wouldn't consider us good enough.

MATSUZO

But he is a man, and a man's position should be higher than his wife's.

YOKICHI

But since he hasn't asked to marry her, how are you going to manage it?

MATSUZO

That's just it. That's what you must manage. Many wealthy men marry their own housemaids, or buy geisha girls for wives. Class difference has nothing to do with marriage. And why shouldn't the manager of a factory marry one of the girls working in the factory? Besides, Oshina is the nicest girl in the lot. The neighbors say so, too.

YOKICHI

But father, I don't want our Oshina treated like a geisha girl. I am poor, but I am a man of honor; and if anyone mistreats my sister, I will kill him. You may as well get these foolish notions out of your head.

MATSUZO

Of course you're a man of honor. That's what I am saying. And that's why you don't need to consider yourself inferior. You can make him marry your sister. Get her to flirt with him.

YOKICHI

No, father! We don't want to do that. You mustn't suggest such things. (*He pauses.*) Where is Oshina, anyway? Hasn't she come home yet?

MATSUZO

She usually gets here before you do, but she hasn't come home yet today.

YOKICHI

She hasn't? Why, all the girls quit work at noon today. She should have been here long before now. Maybe she went to the movies. It worries me to have her hanging around downtown.

MATSUZO

Sure; that's what I say. She's eighteen years old, and needs a man. Unless we get her married, she is apt to go wrong, then our family will be disgraced.

YOKICHI (*angrily*)

I don't like the way she's acting—hanging around downtown and leaving you to do the cooking.

MATSUZO

Don't lose your temper again today. If you do she may leave home the way she did before. Come on; eat plenty of rice and be good.

(*They begin eating. Oshina enters. She is dressed in the simple clothes of a working girl. Yokichi gives her an angry look, and goes on eating his rice. Oshina is frightened, and sits down on the corner of the zashiki.*)

MATSUZO (*scolding her in order to please Yokichi*)

Oshina, where have you been so late? Your brother came home a long time ago. You must behave like a good girl. (*He moves the charcoal stove from in front of Yokichi to a place near Oshina.*) It's cold outside, and you're apt to catch cold. Now warm yourself and eat some supper.

(*Yokichi glares angrily at this show of kindness. He heaps his dish high with rice, then goes and brings the stove back to his own place.*)

MATSUZO

Don't be so mean. You've already warmed yourself, and she has just come in. Let her have the stove. (*He takes it back to Oshina, and says*) You've been a bad girl today, and your brother is mad at you. Be more careful after this.

(*Yokichi has been stirring the fire with the hibashi, or small steel rods belonging to the stove; and now,*)

*in his anger, he forgets what he is holding, and begins
using them in place of chopsticks to eat with. He
burns himself with them. This increases his rage.
He takes them over to the stove, lays them on the fire,
and forces Oshina's hands down on them.)*

YOKICHI

There, young lady, warm yourself! (*He sticks
out his tongue at her.*)

MATSUZO

Now! Don't be so ill-tempered. You might for-
give her this time. And you, Oshina, promise him
that you will be a good girl. He loves you very
much—that's why he is angry. (*He catches sight
of a small parcel wrapped in cloth, which Oshina
has brought home with her.*) What have you got
there? Is that a present for your brother? Why
don't you open it? Let me see. (*He unfolds it
and shows delighted surprise.*) Oh, rice cakes!

(*As Yokichi hears this his face softens, but happen-
ing to look at Oshina, he pretends that he is still angry.*)

MATSUZO

Here! Eat some of this, and make peace with
her.

(*Matsuzo puts the box of rice cakes before Yokichi.
Oshina lowers her head and remains silent.*)

YOKICHI (*pettishly*)

I don't want it. I won't eat anything she brings
home.

MATSUZO

Don't talk that way. Eat this—it is fine. (*He*

THREE MODERN JAPANESE PLAYS

eats.) These are fine cakes. You had better eat
and be good.

YOKICHI (*tempted to eat, but disliking to give in, mutters*)
No sense in her staying out so long. Where have
you been, anyway? (*He takes one rice cake.*)

MATSUZO

Don't say any more about it. (*He hands the box
of cakes to Oshina.*) You want some too, don't
you? And promise you'll come straight home
after this. . . . You like the ones with egg,
don't you? There's one, right there.

OSHINA (*shaking her head*)

I don't want any. I've already eaten.

MATSUZO

You've eaten, you say? Where? (*He looks into
her face.*) Then this is all for your brother, eh?
(*Understandingly*) That's like a good sister. (*He
turns the box over to Yokichi.*) Now, Yokichi, this
is all for you. So eat it, and be nice to her.

YOKICHI (*starts to take another cake, but sees the trademark on the box*)
What! This trademark says "Chidori Restaurant,
Sumiyoshi"! (*Musingly*) The "Chidori" is the
most famous restaurant in Sumiyoshi. That's no
place for a working girl like you. How did you
get there? Who did you go with? (*Severely*)
Who took you out to such a big restaurant? It
wasn't any common man. (*Loudly*) Oshina,
where were you this afternoon, and who was with
you? Speak up, I say! Who took you to Sumiyoshi?

OSHINA (*indifferently*)

Don't you worry about that.

84

YOKICHI

It's my business to worry. Who were you with? You little fool!

MATSUZO

Now, Oshina, you are still a young girl, so you must let him look after you. Tell him who you went with. It must have been some very fine man . . . who?

OSHINA

Oh. . . . (*Casually*) The President took me over there.

YOKICHI

What! (*In astonishment*) The President!

MATSUZO (*to Oshina*)

You mean the President of the Company?

OSHINA (*nodding*)

Yes.

MATSUZO (*happy and excited*)

Yokichi, did you hear that? She went to Sumiyoshi with the President! (*Yokichi stares at Oshina.*) He is in love with her, I'll bet! Didn't I tell you she was the nicest girl in the bunch? Now, Yokichi, you will get a good chance, too. And it's all her doing. Don't you see how grand it is?

YOKICHI (*very angry*)

Father, what are you talking about? The President has a legitimate wife. There's nothing good in it for Oshina. (*To Oshina*) Look here, Oshina; there must be something else. Tell me now, where have you been with him all afternoon? You must have gone somewhere besides the restaurant; it wouldn't take the whole afternoon for you to eat. Where else did you stop? Speak up!

OSHINA (*in a natural manner*)

I haven't done anything wrong. We just rode around in the machine, and he showed me everything.

MATSUZO (*growing more excited*)

Did you hear that? She has been joy-riding! People like us hardly get a ride in an automobile once in a lifetime. That was a great chance for her. I tell you he is in love with her!

YOKICHI (*ignoring his father*)

Look here, Oshina. Lift up your head! Do you realize what he is after, when he takes a common working girl like you joy-riding, and treats you in a big restaurant? You are playing with fire. (*He forces her head back until she looks at him. And then he sees that she is carrying a watch in the bosom of her kimono.*) What's this? A gold watch! (*Now he notices that she wears a diamond ring on her finger.*) And this! A diamond ring! So he gave you these! There's something between you, if he makes you such gifts. Did you stop at a hotel with him? Speak!

MATSUZO

Now, Oshina, if it is true, why don't you tell him? The President is rich, and we can get some money out of him.

YOKICHI

Father, aren't you ashamed! Have you no sense of decency left? What does it matter if he is the President, and a rich man? He has a lawful wife. We are poor folks, but Oshina is a pure girl, and I won't stand for her being abused.

86

MATSUZO

Don't be so self-righteous. That's not the business of poor people like us. If she is attractive to a rich man, that's her good luck. Maybe he will make her his mistress, and give her a good monthly allowance, then she won't need to work any more at the factory, and I can have an easy life too. Don't you see?

YOKICHI (*still angry*)

If you want her to do that, why don't you sell her to a house of prostitution and have done with it? (*Tears come to his eyes.*) Look at me. I have nothing to wear but this old cotton kimono, yet because she is young, I bought her last Christmas a fine new coat. It isn't real silk, but it was the best I could afford. I wanted her to look decent. (*To Oshina*) You don't understand how much I care for you, or you wouldn't hurt me as you do. You're letting your vanity turn you into a plaything for these rich rascals. (*To Matsuzo*) Father, she is your only daughter, and my only sister. How can you say it is good luck for her to be abused? The poorer you get, the lower you sink. (*To Oshina*) You immoral girl, you! (*He kicks her.*)

OSHINA

I tell you, we didn't stop at any hotel. We went to the restaurant to eat, then we rode around awhile and came home.

YOKICHI

You are lying! No man would give you such expensive things just for that.

MATSUZO

But this man is rich. These presents seem very

expensive to us because we are poor; but to him they are like toys that he would buy for a child. We needn't worry about that. She's a nice girl, and he just wanted to show her some kindness.

YOKICHI

Thanks for his kindness! I don't like his motive.

MATSUZO

Oh, you're always making something out of nothing.

YOKICHI

But he isn't generous. He refuses to pay better wages, so why should he want to spend anything merely for the sake of kindness. . . . And if he did, you haven't any reason for accepting his gifts. I am going to return them to him. (*He tries to take the watch and ring from Oshina.*)

MATSUZO

Don't be so foolish! What's the use of returning them? He gave them to her, and she is glad to have them.

YOKICHI

No! She is not in a position to accept these things. Hand them over to me, I tell you! (*He snatches them from her.*)

(*Tomegoro enters. He is a laboring man, about forty years of age, and is dressed in his work-clothes.*)

TOMEGORO (*very excitedly*)

Yokichi! Yokichi! We are out on strike!

YOKICHI

What! Has it come to that at last!

TOMEGORO (*explaining*)

We sent our committee to try to settle things, but

they came back without any satisfactory answer,
so we voted to strike. There is no use trying to
settle things peaceably with that company—they
are too mean.

YOKICHI (*thoughtfully*)

It's easy to start a strike, but hard to finish it.
The company can go a long time before it suffers·
it's us workers who feel it most.

TOMEGORO (*confidently*)

Don't worry about that. It may take a long time,
but we'll burn the company's houses before we
starve to death.

(*A crowd of workers is heard shouting outside.*)

TOMEGORO

Here they come! Here they come!

(*He runs with the others to the door to see the excitement. There is a moment of tenseness in the room.*)

CURTAIN

SCENE II

*The office in Mitsumura's shirt-factory. There is a
flat table in the center of the room, and a desk in the
left corner. Three chairs are placed around the table.
There is a door in the left wall, leading to another
room, and a door at right leading to the street. A
window in the back wall, at center.*

*As the curtain rises Mitsumura is discovered sitting
at the table, center. He is well-dressed, and is engaged
in reading a newspaper. No doubt he is reading the*

*local news section.   His face is concealed from the
audience by the paper.*

*Tamai, his manager, about thirty years of age, and
dressed in American clothes, is seated at the desk,
writing.   There is silence for almost a minute following
the rise of the curtain.   Then Mitsumura bursts into
laughter.*

TAMAI (*turning toward Mitsumura in surprise, and
speaking seriously*)
What's the matter, sir?

MITSUMURA
Well, that rascal! He had a lot of fun.

TAMAI
Whom are you talking about?

MITSUMURA
That Mokichi, who used to be a shipping clerk
and now is worth half a million. Made it during
the war, and is spending it as fast as he made it.

TAMAI
Is that what you meant by "a lot of fun"?

MITSUMURA
Certainly, certainly. That's the most fun a man
can have. The paper says here that last night he
invited all the geisha girls in the Nakano-cho to a
cafe and had a big time—nude dancers and everything. (*Enthusiastically*) There must be about
fifty girls in the Nakano-cho, mustn't there? Think
what a glorious time he had! And only money can
do it. (*Enviously*) Only money.

TAMAI (*with an air of disgust*)
That is abusing the power of money, sir.   But

90

such things seem the only ambitions of Japanese business men. It is the curse of our civilization.

MITSUMURA

But it's not only the business men. How about the army officers and politicians? They have the same ambitions. It's the custom of this country. There is a saying that "All great men are libertines." Why, any real man ought to have five or ten geisha girls around. Of course a man like you, working for someone else, must behave himself. And I must say, you are a good example of that type.

TAMAI

Yes, that is an old tradition in this country, and it is our national shame. Society encourages the idea, and as a result, if any man lives up to it, the newspapers report it as something to be proud of, and no one blames him. Yet they call us one of the civilized nations of the world! I believe we Japanese have the lowest morals in the world.

MITSUMURA

Not at all. Not at all. You have been in America a long while, but most of the time you were in school, so you saw that country through the schoolroom window. Consequently you don't know the real life of America. I've never been there myself, but I've heard Mr. Hayami, President of the Osaka Bank, and Mr. Asai, Representative in the House, who traveled abroad, say that in Europe and America that sort of life is wonderfully developed. The New York underworld is the finest to be seen anywhere. They admired it tremendously.

TAMAI

Of course any country has its dark side, for it is

91

the inevitable product of an imperfect social system. But at the same time, they are trying to improve conditions over there, and they never approve of it morally. Besides, there is no use our excusing ourselves on the ground that other countries suffer from such conditions. It should be the duty of rich people to save girls from such a life. It is not right for men to abuse them for their own pleasure.

MITSUMURA

Of course it is their duty to save them. Unless the rich men spend money on them, how would these poor people be able to live? If everyone was as strict as you are, how would these women get along? The way to save them is to throw money their way.

TAMAI

That is not the way to save them. We must do something more fundamental.

MITSUMURA

How are you going to do that?

TAMAI

Well, in the first place, by changing economic conditions. They do not fall into that way of life because they like it. Most of them sell themselves because of dependent families. They are driven to it by poverty. Therefore, we must give poor people a chance to earn money honestly, and at the same time we must pay them enough to live on. We ought to limit the length of the working-day, so that every laborer would have two hours a day for study. If capitalists would put these things into effect, we would have no poor in the country, and no women would have to sell themselves into slavery.

And we would increase the efficiency of the whole nation. These are real social reforms, and our national prosperity depends upon their adoption.

MITSUMURA

Those are all very good ideas, indeed. But how are we going to make any money out of them? And besides, poor people are those who earn money and are never able to save it. The more they make the more they spend. They overeat and over-drink. They are never satisfied, and they are all lazy. As long as they have money they won't work. And if we were to cut down their working hours, they would use the extra time for gambling, not for studying. And their children are just like them. The women buy luxuries that they can't afford. If you educate them, they grow lazier than ever. I tell you, education won't make them any better. The only way to treat them is to use a whip on them, and get as much work out of them as you can. That is their nature and you can't change them.

TAMAI

If we had given them a chance and they had failed, then they would be to blame; but we haven't given them a chance, so the fault is with society. We ought to start with our own factory and set an example to other companies.

MITSUMURA

That is a good idea, but not a practical one. Social reform is not the object of our company.

TAMAI

But at this very moment our employes are refusing to work without more pay, and if the strike lasts a month we will have a hard time filling our contracts.

MITSUMURA

Well, how are we going to make any profit if we pay higher wages? We might do some good, but we would lose money. There's no sense in running the factory at a loss. If the strike lasts a month, all we have to do is delay filling our orders for another thirty days, and by that time they will be back ready to work. They can't go without eating.

TAMAI

But our contract says the orders must be filled this month.

MITSUMURA

Quite true. There is a clause, though, which provides that in case of strike we are allowed additional time. You look that up.

TAMAI

All right. I will.

(*He goes out at the left. The noise of a mob is heard outside. Chikako, Mitsumura's wife, runs into the office, frightened. She is young, and is dressed richly.*)

CHIKAKO

Help! Help! Oh, I am so frightened. They threw stones at me!

MITSUMURA (*unperturbed*)

That is why I told you not to come here. We are having a strike. And besides, you belong at home; just as I belong here. It is a bad custom we have in this country of mixing the home with the place of business. In Western countries they keep them separate. And that is my principle. You can rule

94

at home, but this office is my territory, and you should keep out. You must realize that I am a big man in the city now, and as you are my wife you must conduct yourself like a lady of position.

CHIKAKO

It's very unkind of you to say that. And it sounds very well for you to speak of home as a sacred place, but the only time you are there is when you have a hangover or are sick in bed. And what's more, its absurd for you to talk about my being the ruler at home.

MITSUMURA

Don't be silly. You know I'd like to stay at home with you every day, but business is too pressing, and that is something I can't help. After all, my hard work is for your sake. When I am rich you will be a high-up lady, and it's time you began acting like one.

CHIKAKO

That's why I am here now. I have come for your congratulations on my becoming a lady of position.

MITSUMURA

What do you mean?

CHIKAKO

I have just been elected vice-president of the W. C. T. U.

MITSUMURA

What! You were elected what!

CHIKAKO

Vice-president of the W. C. T. U. Prince Kuni is president for the whole country, and there are branches in all sections of Japan. I am head of the Osaka branch.

MITSUMURA

Oh, fine! That's fine! I never heard of the organization before, but my friend who has been abroad tells me that in Western countries the women are far ahead of our own women. This feminist movement is getting to be very important.

CHIKAKO

Yes, indeed it is important. And the mission of our society is to wage war on social immorality.

MITSUMURA

A fine idea! Women are so dreadfully immoral these days.

CHIKAKO

No more than men; and our object is to reform the men.

MITSUMURA

Reform the men! Oh, that won't work at all. And besides, such a thing isn't necessary.

CHIKAKO (*ignoring him, continues*)

In the first place, every member of our society keeps an eye on the conduct of her husband.

MITSUMURA

What! Keeps an eye on the conduct of her husband?

CHIKAKO

Yes; very strictly.

MITSUMURA

You are going to keep an eye on my conduct?

CHIKAKO

Yes, indeed. Most strictly!

MITSUMURA

Nonsense! My conduct is above reproach. Why should you watch over me?

CHIKAKO

I know, I know. But it is a rule of our society, and I have to keep my promise as a member.

MITSUMURA

You don't need to keep any such promise. I am all right, and you had better go home.

CHIKAKO

No; I must keep my promise. And you will have to tell me every place you go, and exactly what time you will be home.

MITSUMURA

Well . . . I'll be home . . . when I can.

CHIKAKO

At exactly what time?

MITSUMURA

I can't tell now.

CHIKAKO

But from now on you must set yourself regular hours, and live up to them.

MITSUMURA

Stop talking foolishness!

(*Enter Yokichi.*)

YOKICHI

I want to see the President—you, Mr. Mitsumura.

MITSUMURA

What do you want to see me about? No use asking for a wage increase. The workers' attitude in this present trouble is absolutely selfish and unjust. You will not get a cent from me.

YOKICHI

I am not here to talk about wages. We are out on strike, and we will stay out, even if we starve.

MITSUMURA

All right, then. But what do you want here?

YOKICHI

I have some things to show you—things that are far too expensive for me to have.

MITSUMURA

Why! You fellows are always preaching that all men are equal. And now you're humbling yourself.

YOKICHI

We can discuss that later. Here are some things which should not belong to a poor man, and I wish you to buy them from me.

(*He takes from his breast the watch and diamond ring. Mitsumura starts.*)

CHIKAKO (*delighted*)

Oh, what a lovely diamond ring! And a woman's gold watch!

MITSUMURA (*staring in frightened astonishment*)

How did you get these?

YOKICHI (*with meaning*)

In a very strange way.

MITSUMURA

Strange?

YOKICHI

Yes; I will explain.

MITSUMURA

No; I don't want to hear it.

CHIKAKO (*to her husband*)

But if you are going to buy them from him, you must find out how he got them, and all about it.

YOKICHI

Quite true, lady. As he is going to buy them from me, he must let me explain everything.

MITSUMURA (*vehemently*)

But I don't want to buy them!

CHIKAKO

Why, this is just the kind of watch I have been wanting a long time. It is the very model I asked you to get me. And since Mr. Yokichi is so anxious to sell it, you may as well buy it and help him out.

MITSUMURA

No! No! I don't want any second-hand stuff. It's not good enough for you.

YOKICHI

If you knew the truth about these articles, you couldn't refuse to buy them.

CHIKAKO

It must be a very interesting story. You must tell me all about it.

YOKICHI

Yes, lady; I must tell it. I will tell it. (*He watches Mitsumura.*)

CHIKAKO

Some generous lady must have given them to you to relieve your poverty.

YOKICHI

No; it was not a lady. It was a man, who

calls himself a gentleman, who gave them to my
sister.

(*He still watches Mitsumura. Mitsumura looks
away.*)

CHIKAKO (*eagerly*)

How splendid! Perhaps the gentleman is in love
with your sister. He must be very kind.

YOKICHI

Yes. And I thank him for his kindness, but I
despise his motive.

CHIKAKO

What motive do you mean?

YOKICHI

It is a very common one, to be found in any gentleman. He tried to abuse my sister.

CHIKAKO (*surprised*)

Abuse your sister! Oshina? Why, she is only a
young girl.

YOKICHI

Yes. And the gentleman has a wife. (*He eyes
Mitsumura.*)

CHIKAKO

He has a wife? Oh, how terrible of him, then!

YOKICHI

He is a business man, with a wife who is as fine a
lady as you.

CHIKAKO

How unbelievable! He must be very wicked!
(*To her husband*) My dear, do you believe such
things? That a man with a fine wife would try
to abuse a young girl, and give her these beautiful

presents? What a deceitful person! Surely he cannot be a gentleman.

MITSUMURA

He is not a gentleman; he is a scoundrel, and is not worthy even to breathe the same air as gentlemen.

CHIKAKO

It is shocking!

YOKICHI

Yes, indeed. (*Sarcastically to Mitsumura*) And this scoundrel walks the earth with his head held high; and there are many other gentlemen like him.

CHIKAKO

Who is this man, anyway? I am the new vice-president of the W. C. T. U., and I shall certainly report him to the society. We shall see that he is made an example of.

YOKICHI

You say you will make an example of him? Well, then, I will tell you his name.

CHIKAKO

Of course you must tell me. . . .

MITSUMURA (*interrupting*)

No! Don't mention the name of such a scoundrel in my presence

YOKICHI

You may be right, sir. The names of such villains should not be mentioned before gentlemen like you, who have respectable wives.

MITSUMURA

Never! Never a word! It is disgusting even to hear of it!

YOKICHI

Then I shall say no more about him. But you will buy these articles?

MITSUMURA

Well . . . hm . . . I suppose I have to. How much do you want for them?

YOKICHI

I will make them very reasonable.

MITSUMURA

How much?

YOKICHI (*after looking from one to the other*)

Two thousand yen.

MITSUMURA AND CHIKAKO (*in astonishment*)

Two thousand yen! (*They rise, amazed; then seeing each other, resume their seats in embarrassment.*)

YOKICHI

Don't you think that's very reasonable?

CHIKAKO

Yokichi, you are joking! This watch and this ring never cost as much as that. Why, Mrs. Haruki, a friend of mine, bought the very best watch of this make for five hundred yen, and if you pay a thousand yen for a diamond you can get one ten times as big as this one.

YOKICHI

But, lady, this diamond is of unusual quality. Of course it is small, but it is beautifully cut; and if you put it in a dark room it will give off a blood-red glow. And the ticking of this watch is like the beat of a young girl's heart. If you don't believe it, I will tell you its whole history, then you *will* believe it.

MITSUMURA

Don't bother to explain. I believe all that you say, and that they are very valuable articles. I will pay what you ask.

YOKICHI

You are wise, sir, and seem to understand things perfectly.

CHIKAKO

But it is too much to pay . . .

MITSUMURA (*interrupting*)

No price is too great for things that you wish. You are very dear to me.

YOKICHI

There is no one who thinks as much of his wife as Mr. Mitsumura. (*To Chikako*) You are a very fortunate lady. (*To each of them in turn*) You are the president of a big corporation, and you are the vice-president of the W. C. T. U. You are both wonderful people.

MITSUMURA (*aware of Yokichi's sarcasm*)

Don't talk nonsense! You had better get home. Here are your twc thousand yen. (*He gets the money and reluctantly lays it on the table.*)

YOKICHI

Thank you. (*He takes the money.*) This will help feed the poor workers for a while.

(*Outside are heard the shouts of the workers.*)

YOKICHI

Even poor people can't live without eating, and I have to look after those hungry devils outside. Good-bye, Mr. Mitsumura! Good-bye, madam! (*He leaves.*)

CHIKAKO (*picking up the watch and the ring*)
Two thousand yen. Don't you think that was too much?

MITSUMURA
Oh, this is a very rare gem. And the watch has a magic quality—a mysterious movement like the human heart. The woman who owns it is certain to be loved by her husband, for it has a strange, alluring power.

CHIKAKO
Is that really true? You are not fooling me!

MITSUMURA
It is true. I wouldn't fool you for the world.

CHIKAKO
Sure?

MITSUMURA
Sure. You mustn't doubt me.

CHIKAKO
Oh, I am so glad! You are a wonderful man!
(*They embrace.*)

CURTAIN